THIS COLORING BOOK
BELONGS TO :

Enjoying this colorring book?

Please leave a review because we would love to know your thoughts.

feedback. and opinions to create better paper products for you!

Thank you so much for your support. You are awesome!

HALLOWEEN

SPOOKY
1711-1799
BOO!
R.I.P.

RIP